INTIMA SACRA
A MANUAL OF ESOTERIC DEVOTION

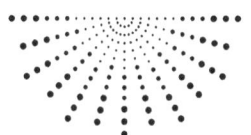

ANNA KINGSFORD

Foreword by
E. MAITLAND
Introduction by
E. M. FORSYTH

"We speak wisdom among the full-grown."

— *I COR.,* **1:6**

CONTENTS

COMPILER'S INTRODUCTION	1
PREFACE	3
THE CREDO	11
THE "LORD'S PRAYER;"	12
CONCERNING HOLY WRIT	13
CONCERNING SIN AND DEATH	15
CONCERNING THE "GREAT WORK," THE REDEMPTION, AND THE SHARE OF CHRIST JESUS THEREIN	18
CONCERNING INSPIRATION	21
CONCERNING THE IMMACULATE CONCEPTION	23
CONCERNING THE FALL	25
CONCERNING IDOLATRY	27
CONCERNING THE NEW ADVENT	28
CONCERNING PRAYER	31
CONCERNING CREATION	32
CONCERNING EVIL	33
CONCERNING ATONEMENT	35
CONCERNING THE HISTORY AND PROGRESS OF THE SOUL	38

CONCERNING RE-INCARNATION	43
GOD'S VOICE OR NOTHING	45
A COUNSEL OF PERFECTION	47
THE THREE VEILS BETWEEN MAN AND GOD	49
HYMN TO PHOIBOS (APOLO)	54
THE HYMN OF APHRODITE	57
HYMN OF LOVE	61
BENEDICTION	67

COMPILER'S INTRODUCTION

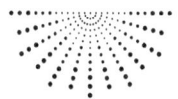

This manual of Esoteric devotion is compiled from the writings of the late Dr. Anna Kingsford for the use of the large and increasing number of devout persons who, whether able or not to recognise under the orthodox presentation of religion the spiritual truths requisite for the sustenance and satisfaction of the soul, earnestly desire an expression of such truths divested of the veils of history, parable, allegory and symbol by which hitherto they have been concealed rather than revealed, and, where perverted or mutilated, restored to their original proper sense and integrity.

The publication is made with the sanction of Mrs. Kingsford's literary collaborator and trustee, Mr. Edward Maitland, who assisted in the selection, and drew up expressly for it the following explanatory statement respecting the derivation and character of the teachings contained in it.

E. M. FORSYTH
LONDON, 1891.

PREFACE

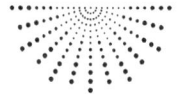

The writings from which this manual is compiled have been recognised and accepted far and vide, with profound joy and thankfulness, by numerous advanced souls, and minds mature and competent for the discernment of spiritual things, as representing a new and inestimable restatement of the original **Gnosis,** or body of transcendental doctrine, which underlay and controlled the expression of the sacred mysteries and scriptures of antiquity, to find its latest formulation and illustration in Christianity. And the recognition thus accorded to them on the ground of their intrinsic character, has the fullest possible confirmation in the manner of their derivation, inasmuch as it was that which has ever been regarded by experts in spiritual science as the true ***modus*** of divine revelation; namely, intuitional perception and recollection, exercised under special illumination of the Spirit, independently of all ordinary processes of mental ratiocination, and immeasurably transcending in results the ability and knowledge of the recipient, or aught that could by any possibility have been obtained by other means. So that the very manner of the acquisition constitutes a demonstration of the essential truth of the doctrine.

The following abstract of the Esoteric doctrine as thus restored will both minister to the comprehension of it as a system of thought, and show that the long sought and sorely needed **Eirenicon** between Faith and Knowledge, Religion and Science, has indeed been at length vouchsafed, in that henceforth—while referred each to its own peculiar plane—the appeal on behalf of both is to one and the same criterion, the **Understanding**.

There is one Being, Self-subsistent, infinite, divine, originally and in itself unmanifest and unindividuate, but impersonal only in the sense of being devoid of limitations, for it is essential and absolute Consciousness. This is God, who is the only real Being. As Spirit, God is a Unity. As Energy and Substance—the necessary constituents of all and every being—God is a Duality: and God becomes manifest through the evolution of His Trinity. Now, Energy and Substance are, respectively, of masculine and feminine potency. Passing into creation, and becoming manifest, God subsists under two modes, the unmanifest and the manifest. But the manifest never exhausts the unmanifest.

Creation, which is the manifestation of God, occurs through the projection, by the divine Will, of the divine Substance into conditions and limitations, whereby it becomes exteriorly cognisable as Matter. Matter is not in itself evil; but being a limitation of Spirit, and therein of God and of consciousness, it is the cause of evil. Such limitation is essential to creation, since creation is manifestation, and manifestation implies gradations and contrasts.

Consisting of the divine Energy and Substance, all things are God as to constituent principles; but because of the limitations necessary to creation, all things are not God as to condition.

But being Spirit, Matter is capable of reverting to the condition of Spirit.

The tendency of Matter to revert to Spirit, or more precisely, of Substance to revert from its material and "created" or "fallen," to its spiritual and original condition, is the cause of Evolution.

Evolution is the manifestation of Inherency; and whereas the inherency in things divine, namely, the Energy and Substance of which all things consist, is itself divine, Evolution reaches its goal, and full manifestation is attained, only when divinity is reached.

That alone which withholds the individual

from the realisation of his proper divine potentialities, is his own will.

Herein lies the mystery called the "Mystery of Godliness"; the mystery, this is, of the "Christ," or the redemption of Spirit from Matter. That mystery is in this wise.

Spirit returns to its essential condition in Soul. Soul is begotten in matter by means of polarisation.

Life is the elaboration of Soul through the varied transformations of matter. Soul is the medium in which Spirit is individuated.

Spirit of itself is diffuse; but enclosed in an envelope of Soul-substance, it becomes an indiffusible personality.

Both Energy and Substance are Spirit; but in speaking of spirit as distinguished from soul, it must be remembered that spirit is always energy and soul is always substance.

The soul is first engendered in the lowest forms of organic life, from which it works upwards, through plants and animals, to man. Once generated and made an individual, it is immortal—unless extinguished through its own perverse will—and passes from one form to another, developing the qualities inherent in its substance, until, in its highest stage, its polarises sufficiently to receive the divine Spirit.

Receiving this Spirit into his soul, the man has, and is, Christ, and is both God and man, Christ being the point of union between the human and the divine.

For, as God is pure Spirit, so is pure Spirit God, and is not the less God because individuated in a human soul, or because, when thus individuated, such soul is invested with a human body. This is the mystery of divine Incarnation. And the secret and method of the Christ is inward purification.

And because the process thereof is interior, it cannot be accomplished by another from without, or by proxy.

The two terms of man's evolution are Creation and Redemption. The first occurs by generation and is of the physical; the second occurs by regeneration and is of the spiritual. The issue of the first is "Adam", the bodily nature or exterior self-hood, "in whom all die". The issue of the second is "Christ", the spiritual nature or interior self-hood, "in whom all have eternal life".

Similarly with the Soul, which, as Substance, is feminine. In the initial human stage of her evolution, she is "Eve" who, succumbing to the sense-nature and lapsing into materiality, becomes "mother" of man degenerate, or "fallen". In the perfected stage, purified from materiality and regaining her proper spiritual condition, she is "Virgin Mary" and "mother" of man regenerate, or "unfallen";–the spiritual, not the physical, self-hood, this is, of the individual concerned, whose soul she is.

Scripture, in such portions of it as, being mystical, represent divine knowledges, sets forth the passage of man and his soul—the latter always under the guise of a woman—from the first to the last stage of their spiritual history, applying to them at each stage a fresh name in accordance with their condition. The entire process has to be undergone by every individual who finally attains to perfection by realising man's highest potentialities. But though all men, even he who is **a** Christ, are saved by Christ, only he is **a** Christ who by accomplishing the process while in the body, manifests the Christ to others, and thereby demonstrates to them their own divine potentialities.

And whereas the process of such regeneration is always in course of accomplishment, and is interior to the individual concerned, Scripture in describing it represents an eternal verity, and the keys to the interpretation of Scripture are the words ***Now*** and ***Within,*** and the creeds founded on Scripture are intelligible and true only when translated into the present tense and referred to the soul.

Now, inasmuch as Regeneration is a long and arduous process, and requires, at least to a certain advanced stage, to be accomplished while in the body, no single earth-life, how prolonged soever, can suffice for it. Wherefore it is necessary that the soul return again and again into the body, as a child to school, to obtain the education, correction, trials and other experiences requisite for edification to the full stature of humanity; and only when it has learnt the lessons the body has to teach, and through conflict with the body has acquired knowledge and strength to overcome the body, and is purged of the tendencies towards materiality which have brought it into and made it subject to the body, is it fitted to dispense with the body and ascend to higher conditions. Hence the doctrine of a multiplicity of earth-lives—which is implicit in Scripture though lost sight of by the churches—is now, in the New Statement, made explicit, being emphatically declared and insisted on as an indispensable and integral article in the faith of the future.

The body of doctrine of which the foregoing is an abstract, is that which in all ages has been known to the initiates of the Sacred Mysteries as the Hermetic Gnosis, and was referred to by Jesus when he charged upon the doctors of the law that they had taken away the key of knowledge—**gnosis,** had not entered in themselves, and had hindered those who would have entered.

It is, therefore, in no sense claimed for the New Statement that it is a new Gospel, but only that it is a new Gospel of Interpretation, and this new only in the sense that it represents the recovery of that which is so old as to have become forgotten. Which said, all has been said that is necessary by way of preface to this book, excepting that this recovery has been made precisely at the period and in the manner long ago predicted in numerous prophecies, both Biblical and extra-Biblical; the coincidence being exact both as regards actual time, and the spiritual condition of church and world.

Edward Maitland

THE CREDO

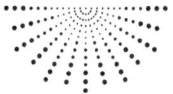

BEING A SUMMARY OF THE SPIRITUAL HISTORY OF THE SONS OF GOD, AND THE MYSTERIES OF THE KINGDOMS OF THE SEVEN SPHERES

I believe in one God; the Father and Mother Almighty; of whose substance are the generations of Heaven and of earth: And in Christ Jesus the Son of God, our Lord; who is conceived of the Holy Ghost; born of the Virgin Mary: suffereth under the world-rulers; is crucified, dead, and buried; who descendeth into hell; who riseth again from the dead; who ascendeth into Heaven, and sitteth at the right hand of God; by whose law the quick and the dead are judged. I believe in the Seven Spirits of God; the Kingdom of Heaven; the communion of the elect; the passing-through of souls; the redemption of the body; the life everlasting; and the Amen.

THE "LORD'S PRAYER;"

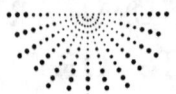

BEING A PRAYER OF THE ELECT FOR INTERIOR PERFECTIONMENT

Our Father-Mother who art in the upper and the within:
Hallowed be thy Name:
Thy Kingdom come:
Thy will be done, in the body as in the spirit:
Give us every day the Communion of the mystical bread:
And perfect us in the power of Thy Sons, according as we give ourselves to perfect others:
And in the hour of temptation deliver us from the hand of Satan:
For Thine are the kingdom, the power, and the glory,
In the life eternal, and in the Amen.

CONCERNING HOLY WRIT

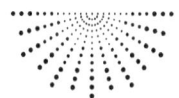

"All Scriptures which are the true Word of God, have a dual interpretation, the intellectual and the intuitional, the apparent and the hidden.

2. For nothing can come forth from God save that which is fruitful.

3. As is the nature of God, so is the Word of God's mouth.

4. The letter alone is barren; the spirit and the letter give life.

5. But that Scripture is the more excellent which is exceeding fruitful and brings forth abundant signification.

6. For God is able to say many things in one, as the perfect ovary contains many seeds in its chalice.

7. Therefore there are in the Scriptures of

God's Word certain writings which, as richly yielding trees, bear more abundantly than others in the self-same holy garden.

8. And one of the most excellent is the history of the generation of the heavens and the earth.

9. For therein is contained in order a genealogy, which has four heads, as a stream divided into four branches, a word exceeding rich.

10. And the first of these generations is that of the Gods.

11. The second is that of the kingdom of heaven.

12. The third is that of the visible world.

13. And the fourth is that of the Church of Christ."

CONCERNING SIN AND DEATH

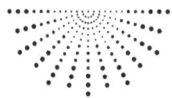

"As is the outer so is the inner: He that worketh is One.

2. As the small is, so is the great: there is one law.

3. Nothing is small and nothing is great in the Divine Economy.

4. If thou wouldst understand the method of the world's corruption, and the condition to which sin hath reduced the work of God,

5. Meditate upon the aspect of a corpse; and consider the method of the putrefaction of its tissues and humours.

6. For the secret of death is the same, whether of the outer or of the inner.

7. The body dieth when the central will of its system no longer bindeth in obedience the elements of its substance.

8. Every cell is a living entity, whether of vegetable or of animal potency.

9. In the healthy body every cell is polarised in subjection to the central will, the Adonai of the physical system.

10. Health, therefore, is order, obedience, and government.

11. But wherever disease is, there is disunion, rebellion, and insubordination.

12. And the deeper the seat of the confusion, the more dangerous the malady, and the harder to quell it.

13. That which is superficial may be more easily healed; or, if need be, the disorderly elements may be rooted out, and the body shall be whole and at unity again.

14. But if the disobedient molecules corrupt each other continually, and the perversity spread, and the rebellious tracts multiply their elements: the whole body shall fall into dissolution, which is death.

15. For the central will that should dominate all the kingdom of the body, is no longer obeyed; and every element is become its own ruler, and hath a divergent will of its own.

16. So that the poles of the cells incline in divers directions; and the binding power which is the life of the body, is dissolved and destroyed.

17. And when dissolution is complete, then follow corruption and putrefaction.

18. Now, that which is true of the physical, is true likewise of its prototype.

19. The whole world is full of revolt; and every element hath a will divergent from God.

20. Whereas there ought to be but one will, attracting and ruling the whole man.

21. But there is no longer brotherhood among you; nor order, nor mutual sustenance.

22. Every cell is its own arbiter; and every member is become a sect.

23. Ye are not bound one to another; ye have confounded your offices, and abandoned your functions.

24. Ye have reversed the direction of your magnetic currents; ye are fallen into confusion, and have given place to the spirit of misrule.

25. Your wills are many and diverse; and every one of you is an anarchy.

26. A house that is divided against itself, falleth.

27. O wretched man; who shall deliver you from this body of death?"

CONCERNING THE "GREAT WORK," THE REDEMPTION, AND THE SHARE OF CHRIST JESUS THEREIN

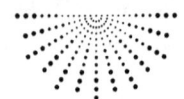

"For this cause is Christ manifest, that he may destroy the works of the devil."

2. In this text of the holy writings is contained the explanation of the mission of the Christ, and the nature of the Great Work.

3. Now the devil, or old serpent, the enemy of God, is that which gives pre-eminence to matter.

4. He is disorder, confusion, distortion, falsification, error. He is not personal, he is not positive, he is not formulated. Whatever God is, that the devil is not.

5. God is light, truth, order, harmony, reason: and God's works are illumination, knowledge, understanding, love, and sanity.

6. Therefore the devil is darkness, falsehood, disorder, discord, ignorance; and his works are confusion, folly, division, hatred and delirium.

7. The devil is therefore the negation of God's Positive. God is I AM; the devil is NOT. He has no individuality and no existence; for he represents the not-being. Wherever God's kingdom is not, the devil reigns.

8. Now the Great Work is the redemption of spirit from matter; that is, the establishment of the kingdom of God.

9. Jesus being asked when the kingdom of God should come, answered, "When two shall be as One, and that which is Without as that which is Within." [1]

10. In saying this he expressed the nature of the Great Work. The Two are spirit and matter: the within is the real invisible; the without is the illusory visible.

11. The kingdom of God shall come when spirit and matter shall be one substance, and the phenomenal shall be absorbed into the real.

12. His design was therefore to destroy the dominion of matter, and to dissipate the devil and his works.

13. And this he intended to accomplish by proclaiming the knowledge of the Universal Dissolvent, and giving to men the keys of the kingdom of God.

14. Now the kingdom of God is within us; that is, it is interior, invisible, mystic, spiritual.

15. There is a power by means of which the outer may be absorbed into the inner.

16. There is a power by means of which matter may be ingested into its original substance.

17. He who possesses this power is Christ, and he has the devil under foot.

18. For he reduces chaos to order, and indraws the external to the centre.

19. He has learnt that matter is illusion, and that spirit alone is real.

20. He has found his own central point: and all power is given unto him in heaven and on earth.

---

1. ***Epistle of S. Clement.***

CONCERNING INSPIRATION

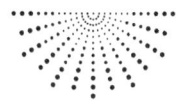

1. You ask the method and nature of Inspiration, and the means whereby God revealeth the Truth.

2. Know that there is no enlightenment from without: the secret of things is revealed from within.

3. From without cometh no Divine Revelation: but the Spirit within beareth witness.

4. Think not I tell you that which you know not: for except you know it, it cannot be given to you.

5. To him that hath it is given, and he hath the more abundantly.

6. None is a prophet save he who knoweth: the instructor of the people is a man of many lives.

7. Inborn knowledge and the perception of

things, these are the sources of revelation: the soul of the man instructeth him, having already learned by experience.

8. Intuition is inborn experience: that which the soul knoweth of old and of former years.

9. And Illumination is the Light of Wisdom, whereby a man perceiveth heavenly secrets.

10. Which Light is the Spirit of God within the man, showing unto him the things of God.

11. Do not think that I tell you anything you know not: all cometh from within: the Spirit that informeth is the Spirit of God in the prophet.

13. The spirit of the prophet beholdeth God with open eyes. If he fall into a trance his eyes are open, and his interior man knoweth what is spoken by him.

14. But when a man speaketh that which he knoweth not, he is obsessed (...)

15. Of such beware, for they speak many lies (...).

16. Inspiration may indeed be medium-ship, but it is conscious; and the knowledge of the prophet instructeth him.

CONCERNING THE IMMACULATE CONCEPTION

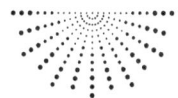

The Immaculate Conception is none other than the prophecy of the means whereby the universe shall at last be redeemed. Maria–the sea of limitless space–Maria the Virgin, born herself immaculate and without spot, of the womb of the ages shall in the fulness of time bring forth the perfect Man who shall redeem the race. He is not one man, but ten thousand times ten thousand, the Son of Man, who shall overcome the limitations of matter and the evil which is the result of the materialization of spirit. His Mother is spirit, his Father is spirit, yet he is himself incarnate; and how then shall he overcome evil and restore matter to the condition of spirit? By force of love. It is love which is the centripetal power of the universe; it is by love that all creation returns into the bosom of God. The force which projected all things is Will; and will is the centrifugal power of Universe.

Will alone could not overcome the evil which results from the limitations of matter; but it shall be overcome in the end by sympathy, which is the knowledge of God in others–the recognition of the Omnipresent Self. This is love. And it is with the children of the Spirit, the servants of love, that the dragon of matter makes war. (...)

All that is true is spiritual. (...) For matter shall cease, and all that is of it, but the Word of the Lord shall remain for ever. If any dogma be true and yet seem to you to have a material signification, know that you have not solved it. That which is true, is for spirit alone.

CONCERNING THE FALL

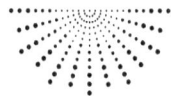

"Now the gift of God is eternal life through Jesus Christ our Lord." "For as in the earthly and rebellious Adam we die; so in the Christ we are alive for evermore." That is, that inasmuch as by disobedience to the Divine Will the soul brings on itself dissolution and eternal death; so, when it is regenerate and strives continually to attain, the Christ nature, it obtains thereby eternal life. For it arises necessarily out of the law of the universe that nothing can continue to exist which is out of harmony with the Divine Central Will. Now, the nature which is in most perfect harmony with the Divine Will is the Christ-nature. Wherefore, of the redeemed universe the perfect chord is, Thy Will be done.

For apart from God, Who is its life, the soul is nothing. And this knowledge of her shameful condition is all the soul gains by rebellion. And so the lesson to the soul is this:—If thou disunite thyself from God and make thy desire earthwards, thou art as the dust of the ground, and must die the death of the body. But if thou desire only God and make God's law thy will, and its accomplishment thy delight, thou becomest as God and hast eternal life.

CONCERNING IDOLATRY

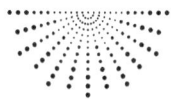

"To make an Idol is to materialize spiritual Mysteries. The Priests were Idolaters, who, coming after Moses and committing to writing those things which he by word of mouth had delivered unto Israel, replaced the true things signified, by their material symbols, and shed innocent blood on the pure altars of the Lord.

"They also are Idolaters who understand the things of sense where the things of the Spirit are alone implied (...). Idolatry is materialism, the common and original sin of men, which replaces Spirit by Appearance, Substance by Illusion (...). It is that false Fruit which attracts the outer Senses, the bait of the Serpent in the beginning of the World."

CONCERNING THE NEW ADVENT

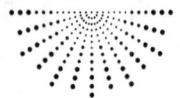

"The token whereby the approach of the End should be known, was to be the spectacle of the "abomination of desolation standing in the holy place." Jesus, recalling this prophecy, foretold the same event, and warned the elect in mystic phrase, thus to be interpreted:—

"When, therefore, ye shall see matter exalted to the holy place of God and the soul, and made the all and in all of existence;

"Then let the spiritual Israel betake themselves to the hills where alone salvation is to be found, even the heights and fastnesses of the divine life.

"And let him who has overcome the body, beware lest he return to the love of the flesh, or seek the things of the world.

"Neither let him who is free from the body, become again re-incarnate.

"And woe to the soul whose travail is yet unaccomplished, and which has not yet become weaned from the body.

"And beseech God that these things find you not at a season either of spiritual depression and feebleness, or of spiritual repose and unwatchfulness.

"For the tribulation shall be without parallel;

"And such that except those days shall be few in number, escape from the body would be impossible.

"But for the elect's sake they shall be few.

"And if any shall then declare that here, or there, the Christ has appeared as a person, believe it not. For there shall arise delusive apparitions and manifestations, together with great signs and marvels, such as might well deceive even the elect. Remember, I have told you beforehand. Wherefore, if they shall say unto you, Behold he is in the desert, whether of the East or of the West,–join him not. Or, Behold he is in darkened rooms and secret assemblies,–pay no regard.

"For, like lightning coming out of the East and illuminating the West, so shall be the world's spiritual awakening to the recognition of the Divine in Humanity.

"But wheresoever the dead carcase of error remains, around it, like vultures, will gather both deceivers and deceived.

"And upon them, the profane there shall be

darkness; the Spirit shall be quenched and the soul extinct; and there shall be no more any light in heaven, or in heavenly science any truth and meaning. And the power of heaven upon men shall be shaken.

"Then shall appear the new sign, the Man in Heaven, upon the rain-clouds of the last chrism and mystery, with great power and glory." [1]

---

1. Indicated in the Zodiacal sign *Aquarius* which succeeds *Pisces* the sign of the Christian dispensation. Hence the significance of *Mark* XIV:13 and *Luke* XXII:10.

CONCERNING PRAYER

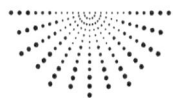

"Prayer means the intense direction of the will and desire towards the Highest; an unchanging intent to know nothing but the Highest. (...) The command always is, "To labour is to pray;" "To ask is to receive;" "To knock is to have the door opened." When you think inwardly, pray intensely, and imagine centrally, then you converse with God.

"So long as Moses held up his hands towards heaven, the Israelites prevailed. When he dropped them, then the Amalekites."

CONCERNING CREATION

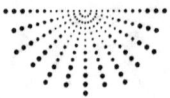

"Creation, or the putting forth of things, is not to be thought of as an act once accomplished and then ended. For the celestial Olympus is continually creating and continually becoming. God never ceases giving of God for God's creatures. This also is the Mystery of the divine Incarnation and Oblation. The celestial substance is continually individualizing itself that it may build itself up into one perfect individual. Thus is the circle of life accomplished, and thus its ends meet the one with the other."

CONCERNING EVIL

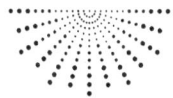

"Understand that evil is the result of creation. For creation is the projection of spirit into matter, and with this projection came the first germ of evil. We would have you know that there is no such thing as purely spiritual evil, but that evil is the result of the materialization of spirit. If you examine carefully all the various forms of evil, you will see that every one is the result of the limitations of matter. Falsehood is the limitation of the faculty of perception; selfishness is the result of the limitation of the power to perceive that the whole Universe is but the larger Self; and so of all the rest. It is then true that God created evil; but yet it is true that God is Spirit, and being Spirit is incapable of evil. Evil is then purely and solely the result of the materialization of God. (…)

"God is perception itself God is universal percipience. God is both that which sees and that which is seen. If we could see all, hear all, touch all, and so forth, there would be no evil, for evil comes of the limitation of perception. Such limitation was necessary if God was to produce aught other than God. Aught other than God must be less than God. Without evil, therefore, God would have remained alone. All things are God according to the measure of the Spirit in them.

"And nearest of all to God is woman" (as type of the feminine or Love aspect of the Divine Nature).

"Any act or desire of the body that does not profit the mind, that is sensuality."

CONCERNING ATONEMENT

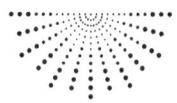

"Only where love is perfect is sympathy perfect, and only where sympathy is perfect can one die for another.

Wherefore the Son of God says, "The wrongs of others wound me and the stripes of others fall upon my flesh. I am smitten with the pains of all creatures, and my heart is pierced with their hearts. There is no offence done and I suffer not. Nor any wrong and I am not hurt thereby. For my heart is in the breast of every creature, and my blood is in the veins of all flesh. I am wounded in my right hand for man, and in my left hand for woman–in my right and left feet for the beasts of the earth and the creatures of the deep, and in my heart for all." The Crucifix, then, is the divinest of symbols, because it is the emblem of Christ and token of God with man. It is the allegory of the doctrine of Pantheism that man becomes perfect–the soul becomes God–through suffering. He who is wise understands; and he who understands is initiated; and he who is initiated loves; and he who loves knows, and he who knows is purified. And the pure behold God and comprehend the Divine with the mystery of pain and of death. And because the Son of God loves he is powerful, and the power of love redeems. He being lifted up draws all men unto him."

"And this is the Atonement of Christ and perpetual sacrifice of the Son of God. Believe and thou shalt be saved; for he that believeth is changed from the image of death to life. And he that believeth sinneth no more and oppresseth no more. For he loveth as Christ hath loved, and is in God and God in him. The blood of Christ cleanseth from all sin, not by the purchase of pardon with another's gold, but because the love of God hath changed the life of the sinner. The penitent saves himself by suffering, sorrow, and amendment. By these he rises and his life is redeemed. And it is the Christ that redeems him by giving his heart's blood for him. It is Christ in him who takes his infirmities and bears his sorrows in his own body on the tree. And the same which was true of old is true to-day, and forever. Christ Jesus is crucified continually in each one until the

Kingdom of God come. For wherever is sin are suffering, death and oppression; and where these are, the Christ shall be manifest, and by love shall labour and die and redeem."

CONCERNING THE HISTORY AND PROGRESS OF THE SOUL

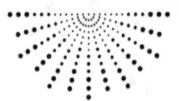

"Souls[1] (...) work upwards from plants and animals to man. In man they attain their perfection and the power to dispense altogether with material bodies. Their ability to do this is the cause and consequence of their perfection. And it is the attainment of this that is the object of the culture of the soul—the object, that is, of religion. Spirit alone is good, is God. Matter is that whereby spirit is limited, and is therein the cause of evil; for evil is the limitation of good. Wherefore, to escape from matter and its limitations and return to the condition of spirit is to be superior to the liability to evil. Formerly the way of escape for human souls was more open than now, and the path clearer. Because although ignorance of intellectual things abounded, especially among the poorer folk, yet the knowledge of divine things and the light of faith were stronger and purer. The ***anima bruta,*** or earthly mind, was less strongly defined and fixed, so that the ***anima divina,*** or heavenly mind, subsisted in more open conditions. Wherefore the souls of those ages of the world, not being enchained to earth as they are now, were enabled to pass more quickly through their avatârs; and but few incarnations sufficed where now many are necessary. For in these days the mind's ignorance is weighted by materialism instead of being lightened by faith; and the soul is sunk to earth by love of the body, by atheism, and by excessive care for the things of sense. And being crushed thereby, it lingers long in the atmosphere of earth, seeking many fresh lodgments, and so multiplies bodies, the circumstances of each of which are influenced by the use made of the previous one.

"For every man makes his own fate, and nothing is truer than that Character is Destiny. It is by their own hands that the lines of some are cast in pleasant places, of some in vicious, and of some in virtuous ones, so that there is nothing arbitrary or unjust. But in what manner soever a soul conduct itself in one incarnation, by that conduct, by that order of thought and habit, it builds for itself its destiny in a future incarnation. For the soul is enchained by these pre-natal influences, which irresistibly force it into a new nativity at the time of such conjunction of planets and signs as oblige it into certain courses and incline it strongly thereto. But if the soul oppose itself to these influences and adopt some other course—as it well may to its own real advantage—it brings itself under a "curse" for such period as the planets and ruling signs of that incarnation have power. But though this means misfortune in a worldly sense, it is true fortune for the soul in a spiritual sense. For the soul is therein striving to atone and make restitution for the evil done in its own past; and thus striving, it advances towards higher and happier conditions. Wherefore man is, strictly, his own creator, in that he makes himself and his conditions according to the tendencies he encourages. The process of such reformation, however, may be a long one. For tendencies encouraged for ages cannot be cured in a single life-time, but may require ages for their cure. And herein is a reflection to make us as patient towards the faults of others, as it ought to make us impatient of our own.

"The doctrine of the soul is embodied in the parable of the talents as thus explained:–Into the soul of the individual is breathed the Spirit of God, divine, pure, and without blemish. It is God. And the individual has in his earth-life to nourish that Spirit, and feed it as a flame with oil. When you put oil into a lamp the essence passes into and becomes flame. So is it with the soul of him who nourishes the Spirit. It grows gradually pure and **becomes** the spirit. By this means the Spirit becomes the richer. And as in the parable of the talents, where God has given five talents, man gives back ten, or he returns nothing, and perishes."

"Some oils are finer and more combustible than others. The finest is that of the soul of the poet: and in such a medium the flame of God's Spirit burns more clearly and powerfully and brightly, so that sometimes mortal eyes can hardly endure its lustre. Of such an one the soul is filled with holy rapture. He sees as no other man sees, and the atmosphere about him is enkindled. His soul becomes transmuted into flame; and when the lamp of his body is shattered, his flame mounts and soars and is united to the Divine Fire." [2]

[3] "The reason why the doctrine of Metempsychosis is not put forward as an article of faith in the Christian dispensation appears to be because there is no more death or birth for the man who is united with God in Christ. The Christian religion was addressed to this end, and he who enters the kingdom of heaven is saved for ever from that of earth. But very few realise this blessed state, therefore says the Lord—"Few there be that find it." Not, assuredly, that all the majority are lost, but that they return to the necessary conditions again and again till they find it. When once the life of union is achieved the wheel of existence ceases to revolve. Now the Church takes it for granted that every Christian desires in this existence to attain to

union, such union with Christ being, in fact, the sole subject and object of Christian faith and doctrine. Therefore, of course, she does not preach the Metempsychosis. But as a matter of fact very few so-called Christians do attain union; therefore they return until the capacity for union is developed. Such development must be reached in mundane conditions; the cleansing fires of an afterworld are incapable of more than purification, they do not supply the necessary conditions for evolution, found only and granted only in this life. Now the dispensation of Christ is the highest there is, because regeneration begins for the Christian in the interior principle and works outwardly. In other dispensations it begins outwardly and works towards the interior."

"Buddha, in whose system the Metempsychosis is most conspicuous, is in the mind; Christ is in the soul. Therefore Buddha preaches no soul, and Christ preaches no mind. "Who are born," says St. John, speaking of the servants of Christ, "not of blood, nor of the will of the flesh, nor of the will of man, but of God."

---

1. *The Perfect Way*. Lect. 2, Part 3.
2. *The Story of Anna Kingsford and Edward Maitland and of the New Gospel of Interpretation*. Chapter IV, p. 119.
3. *The Credo of Christendon*. Chapter 13, p. 223

CONCERNING RE-INCARNATION

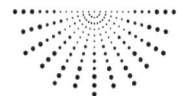

"There are three conditions under which the soul returns to the man's form, and they are these: –

- 1st. When the work which the Spirit proposes to accomplish is of a nature unsuitable to the female form.
- 2nd. When the Spirit has failed to acquire in the degree necessary to perfection, certain special attributes of the male character.
- 3rd. When the Spirit has transgressed and gone back in the path of perfection by degrading the womanhood it had attained.

In the first of these cases its return to the male

form is outward and superficial only. Therefore is it—though a woman—clothed in a man's body that it may be enabled to do the work set before it.

The second case is that of a soul, who, having been a woman perhaps many times, has acquired more aptly and readily the higher qualities of womanhood than the lower qualities of manhood. Such a soul is lacking in energy, in resoluteness, in that particular attribute of the Spirit which the prophet ascribes to the Lord when he says, "The Lord is a man of war." Therefore the soul is put back into a man's form to acquire the qualities yet lacking.

The third case is that of the backslider who, having nearly attained perfection, perhaps even touched it, degrades and soils his white robe and is put back into the lower form again. These are the common cases, for there are few women who are worthy to be women."

GOD'S VOICE OR NOTHING

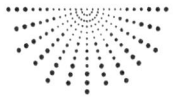

"After Buddha had been ten years in retirement, certain sages sent their disciples to him asking him "What dost thou claim to be, Gotama?"

Buddha answered them, "I claim to be nothing." Ten years afterwards they sent again to him asking him the same question, and again Buddha answered: "I claim to be nothing." Then after yet another ten years had passed they sent a third time asking, "What dost thou claim to be, Gotama?"

And Buddha replied, "I claim to be the utterance of the most High God."

Then they said to him, "How is this that hitherto thou hast proclaimed thyself to be nothing, and now thou declarest thyself to be the very utterance of God?"

Buddha answered, "Either I am nothing or I am the very utterance of God; for between these two all is silence."

A COUNSEL OF PERFECTION

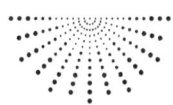

I dreamed that I was in a large room, and there were in it seven persons, all men, sitting at one long table; and each of them had before him a scroll, some having books also; and all were grey-headed and bent with age save one, and this was a youth of about twenty, without hair on his face. One of the aged men who had his finger on a place in a book open before him, said: -

"This spirit who is of our order writes in this book, 'Be ye perfect therefore, as your Father in heaven is perfect.' How shall we understand this word 'perfection'?"

And another of the old men looking up answered, "It must mean Wisdom, for wisdom is the sum of perfection."

And another old man said, "That cannot be; for no creature can be wise as God is wise. Where is he among us who could attain to such a state? That which is part only cannot comprehend the whole. To bid a creature to be wise as God is wise, would be a mockery."

Then a fourth old man said:—"It must be Truth that is intended. For truth only is perfection."

But he who sat next the last speaker answered, "Truth also is partial; for where is he among us who shall be able to see as God sees?"

And the sixth said, "It surely must be justice; for this is the whole of righteousness."

And the old man who had spoken first answered him: "Not so; for Justice comprehends vengeance, and it is written that vengeance is the Lord's alone."

Then the young man stood up with an open book in his hand and said, "I have here another record of one who likewise heard these words. Let us see whether his rendering of them can help us to the knowledge we seek." And he found a place in the book and read aloud:—

> *"Be ye merciful, even as your Father is merciful."*

THE THREE VEILS BETWEEN MAN AND GOD

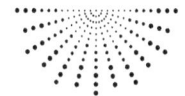

"A golden chalice, like those used in Catholic rites, but having three linings, was given to me in my sleep by an Angel. These linings, he told me, signified the three degrees of the heavens,–purity of life, purity of heart, and purity of doctrine. Immediately afterwards there appeared to me a great dome-covered temple, Moslem in style, and on the threshold of it a tall angel clad in white linen, who with an air of command was directing a party of men engaged in destroying and throwing into the street numerous crucifixes, bibles, prayer-books, altar-utensils, and other sacred emblems. As I stood watching, somewhat scandalised at the apparent sacrilege, a voice at a great height in the air, cried with startling distinctness, "All the idols He shall utterly destroy!" Then the same voice, seeming to ascend still higher, cried to me, "Come hither and see!" Immediately it appeared to me that I was lifted up by my hair and carried above the earth. And suddenly there arose in mid-air the apparition of a man of majestic aspect, in an antique garb, and surrounded by a throng of prostrate worshippers. At first the appearance of this figure was strange to me; but while I looked intently at it, a change came over the face and dress, and I thought I recognised Buddha,–the Messiah of India. But scarcely had I convinced myself of this, when a great voice, like a thousand voices shouting in unison cried to the worshippers: "Stand upright on your feet:–Worship God only!" And again the figure changed, as though a cloud had passed before it, and now it seemed to assume the shape of Jesus. Again I saw the kneeling adorers, and again the mighty voice cried, "Arise! Worship God only!" The sound of this voice was like thunder, and I noted that it had seven echoes. Seven times the cry reverberated, ascending with each utterance as though mounting from sphere to sphere. Then suddenly I fell through the air, as though a hand had been withdrawn from sustaining me: and again touching the earth, I stood within the temple I had seen in the first part of my vision. At its east end was a great altar, from above and behind which came faintly a white and beautiful light, the radiance of which was arrested and obscured by a dark curtain suspended from the dome before the altar. And the body of the temple, which, but for the curtain, would have been fully illumined, was plunged in gloom, broken only by the fitful gleams of a few half-expiring oil-lamps, hanging here and there from the vast cupola. At the right of the altar stood the same tall angel I had before seen on the temple threshold, holding in his hand a smoking censer. Then, observing that he was looking earnestly at me, I said to him: "Tell me, what curtain is this before the light, and why is the temple in darkness?" And he answered, "This veil is not One, but Three; and the Three are Blood, Idolatry, and the Curse of Eve. And to you it is given to withdraw them; be faithful and courageous; the time has come." Now the first curtain was red, and very heavy; and with a great effort I drew it aside, and said, "I have put away the veil of blood from before Thy Face. Shine, O Lord God!" But a voice from behind the folds of the two remaining coverings answered me, "I cannot shine, because of the idols." And lo, before me a curtain of many colours, woven about with all manner of images, crucifixes, madonnas, Old and New Testaments, prayer-books, and other religious symbols, some strange and hideous like the idols of China and Japan, some beautiful like those of the Greeks and Christians. And the weight of the curtain was like lead, for it was thick with gold and silver embroideries. But with both hands I tore it away, and cried, "I have put away the idols from before Thy Face. Shine, O Lord God!" And now the light was clearer and brighter. But yet before me hung a third veil, all of black; and upon it was traced in outline the figure of four lilies on a single stem inverted, their cups opening downwards. And from behind this veil the voice answered me again, "I cannot shine, because of the curse of Eve." Then I put forth all my strength, and with a great will rent away the curtain, crying, "I have put away her curse from before Thee. Shine, O Lord God!"

And there was no more a veil, but a landscape, more glorious and perfect than words can paint, a garden of absolute beauty, filled with trees of palm, and olive, and fig, rivers of clear water and lawns of tender green; and distant groves and forests framed about by mountains crowned with snow; and on the brow of their shining peaks a rising sun, whose light it was I had seen behind the veils. And about the sun, in mid-air hung white misty shapes of great angels, as clouds at morning float above the place of dawn. And beneath, under a mighty tree of cedar, stood a white elephant, bearing in his golden houdah a beautiful woman robed as a queen, and wearing a crown. But while I looked, entranced, and longing to look for ever, the garden, the altar, and the temple were carried up from me into Heaven. Then as I stood gazing upwards, came again the voice, at first high in the air, but falling earthwards as I listened. And behold, before me appeared the white pinnacle of a minaret, and around and beneath it the sky was all gold and red with the glory of the rising sun. And I perceived that now the voice was that of a solitary Muezzin standing on the minaret with uplifted hands and crying:–

"Put away Blood from among you!
Destroy your Idols!
Restore your Queen!"

And straightway a voice, like that of an infinite multitude, coming as though from above and around and beneath my feet,–a voice like a wind rising upwards from caverns under the hills to their loftiest far-off heights among the stars, responded–

"Worship God alone!"

HYMN TO PHOIBOS (APOLO)

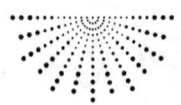

1. "Strong art thou and adorable, Phoibos Apollo, who bearest life and healing on thy wings, who crownest the year with thy bounty, and givest the spirit of thy divinity to the fruits and precious things of all the worlds.

2. Where were the bread of the initiation of the sons of God, except thou bring the corn to ear; or the wine of their mystical chalice, except thou bless the vintage?

3. Many are the angels who serve in the courts of the spheres of heaven: but thou, Master of Light and of Life, art followed by the Christs of God.

4. And thy sign is the sign of the Son of Man in heaven, and of the Just made perfect;

5. Whose path is as a shining light, shining

more and more unto the innermost glory of the day of the Lord God.

6. Thy banner is blood-red, and thy symbol is a milk-white lamb, and thy crown is of pure gold.

7. They who reign with thee are the Hierophants of the celestial mysteries; for their will is the will of God, and they know as they are known.

8. These are the sons of the innermost sphere; the Saviours of men, the Anointed of God.

9. And their name is Christ Jesus, in the day of their initiation.

10. And before them every knee shall bow, of things in heaven and of things on earth.

11. They are come out of great tribulation; and are set down for ever at the right hand of God.

12. And the Lamb, which is in the midst of the seven spheres, shall give them to drink of the river of living water.

13. And they shall eat of the tree of life, which is in the centre of the garden of the kingdom of God.

14. These are thine, O Mighty Master of Light; and this is the dominion which the Word of God appointed thee in the beginning.

15. In the day when God created the light of all the worlds, and divided the light from the darkness.

16. And God called the light Phoibos, and the darkness God called Python.

17. Now the darkness was before the light, as the night forerunneth the dawn.

18. These are the evening and the morning of the first cycle of the Mysteries.

19. And the glory of that cycle is as the glory of seven days; and they who dwell therein are seven times refined;

20. Who have purged the garment of the flesh in the living waters;

21. And have transmuted both body and soul into spirit, and are become pure virgins.

22. For they were constrained by love to abandon the outer elements, and to seek the innermost which is undivided, even the Wisdom of God.

23. And Wisdom and Love are One."

THE HYMN OF APHRODITE

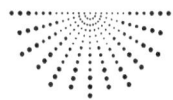

(1)

"I AM the dawn, daughter of heaven and of the deep: the sea-mist covers my beauty with a veil of tremulous light.

2. I am Aphrodite, the sister of Phoibos, opener of heaven's gates, the beginning of wisdom, the herald of the perfect day.

3. Long had darkness covered the deep: the soul of all things slumbered: the valleys were filled with shadows: only the mountains and the stars held commune together.

4. There was no light on the ways of the earth: the rolling world moved outward on her axe: gloom and mystery shrouded the faces of the Gods.

5. Then from out the deep I arose, dispeller of

night: the firmament of heaven kindled with joy beholding me.

6. The secrets of the waters were revealed: the eyes of Zeus looked down into the heart thereof.

7. Ruddy as wine were the depths: the raiment of earth was transfigured; as one arising from the dead She arose, full of favour and grace.

(2)

8. Of God and the soul is love born: in the silence of twilight; in the mystery of sleep.

9. In the fourth dimension of space; in the womb of the heavenly principle; in the heart of the man of God;–there is love enshrined.

10. Yea, I am before all things: desire is born of me: I impel the springs of life inward unto God: by me the earth and heavens are drawn together.

11. But I am hidden until the time of the day's appearing: I lie beneath the waters of the sea, in the deeps of the soul: the bird of night seeth me not, the herds in the valleys, nor the wild goat in the cleft of the hill.

12. As the fishes of the sea am I covered: I am secret and veiled from sight as the children of the deep.

13. That which is occult hath the fish for a symbol; for the fish is hidden in darkness and si-

lence: he knoweth the secret places of the earth, and the springs of the hollow sea.

14. Even so love reacheth to the uttermost: so find I the secret of all things; having my beginning and my end in the Wisdom of God.

15. The Spirit of Counsel is begotten in the soul; even as the fish in the bosom of the waters.

16. From the sanctuary of the deep love ariseth: salvation is of the sea.

(3)

17. I am the crown of manifold births and deaths: I am the interpreter of mysteries and the enlightener of souls.

18. In the elements of the body is love imprisoned lying asleep in the caves of Iacchos; in the crib of the oxen of Demeter.

19. But when the day-star of the soul ariseth over the earth, then is the epiphany of love.

20. Therefore until the labour of the third day be fulfilled, the light of love is unmanifest.

21. Then shall l unlock the gates of dawn; and the glory of God shall ascend before the eyes of men.

(4)

22. The secret of the angel Anael is at the heart of the world: the "Song of God" is the sound of the stars in their courses.

23. O love, thou art the latent heat of the earth; the strength of the wine; the joy of the orchard and the cornfield: thou art the spirit of song and laughter, and of the desire of life.

24. By thee, O goddess, pure-eyed and golden, the sun and the moon are revealed: love is the counselor of heaven.

25. Cloud and vapour melt before thee: thou unveilest to earth the rulers of the immeasurable skies.

26. Thou makest all things luminous: thou discoverest all deeps,

27. From the womb of the sea to the heights of heaven; from the shadowy abyss to the throne of the Lord.

28. Thy beloved is as a ring-dove, wearing the ensign of the spirit, and knowing the secrets thereof.

29. Fly, fly, O Dove; the time of spring cometh; in the far east the dawn ariseth; she hath a message for thee to bear from earth to heaven."

HYMN OF LOVE

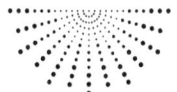

A DISCOURSE OF THE COMMUNION OF SOULES, AND OF THE USES OF LOVE BETWEEN CREATURE AND CREATURE: BEING PART OF THE GOLDEN BOOK OF VENUS

"1. Herein is Love's Secret, and the Mysterie of the Communion of Saintes.

2. Love redeemeth, Love lifteth up, Love enlighteneth, Love advanceth Soules.

3. Love dissolveth not, neither forgetteth; for she is of the Soule and hath everlasting Remembrance.

4. Verilie Love is doubly blessed; for She enricheth both Giver and Receiver.

5. Thou who lovest givest of thyself to thy Beloved, and he is dowered withal.

6. And if any Creature whom thou lovest suffereth Death and departeth from thee;

7. Fain wouldst thou give of thine Heartes Blood to have him live always; to sweeten the

Changes before or to lift him to some happie Place.

8. Thou droppest teares on the broken Body of thy Beloved; thy Desire goeth after him, and thou criest unto his Ghoste, –

9. "O Dearest! Would God that I might be with thee where now thou art, and know what now thou doest!

10. "Would God that I might still guard and protect thee; that I might defend thee from all Pain, and Wrong and Affliction!

11. "But what Manner of Change is before thee I know not; neither can mine Eyes follow thy Steppes.

12. "Many are the Lives set before thee, and the Yeares, O Beloved, are long and weary that shall part us!

13. "Shall I knowe thee again when I see thee, and will the Spirit of God say to thee in that day, 'This is thy Beloved?'

14. "O Soule of my Soule! Would God I were one with thee, even though it were in death!

15. "Thou hast all of my Love, my Desire, and my Sorrowe; yea, my Life is mingled with thine, and is gone forth with thee!

16. "Visit me in Dreames; comfort me in the Night-watches; let my Ghoste meet thine in the Land of Shadows and of Sleep!

17. "Every nighte with fervent Longing will I

seek thee; Persephone and Slumber shall give me back the Past.

18. "Yea, Death shall not take thee wholly from me; for Part of me is in thee, and where thou goest, Dearest, there my Hearte followeth!"

19. So weepest thou and lamentest, because the Soul thou lovest is taken from thy Sight.

20. And Life seemeth to thee a Bitter Thing; yea, thou cursest the Destiny of all living Creatures.

21. And thou deemest thy Love of no avail, and thy Teares as idle Droppes.

22. Behold, Love is a Ransome, and the Teares thereof are Prayeres.

23. And if thou have lived purely, thy fervent Desire shall be counted Grace to the Soule of thy Dead.

24. For the burning and continual Prayere of the Juste availeth much.

25. Yea, thy Love shall enfold the Soule which thou lovest; it shall be unto him a wedding Garment and a Vesture of Blessing.

26. The Baptisme of thy Sorrowe shall baptize thy Dead, and he shall rise because of it.

27. Thy Prayeres shall lift him up, and thy Teares shall encompasse his Steppes; thy Love shall be to him a Light shining upon the upward Waye.

28. And the Angels of God shall say unto him,

"O happie Soule that art so well beloved; that art made so strong with all these Teares and Sighs.

29. "Praise the Father of Spirits therefore, for this great Love shall save thee many Incarnations.

30. "Thou art advanced thereby; thou art drawn aloft and carried upward by Cordes of Grace."

31. For in such wise do Soules profit one another and have Communion, and receive and give Blessing, the Departed of the Living, and the Living of the Departed.

32. And so much the more as the Hearte within them is clean, and the Waye of their Intention is innocent in the Sight of God.

33. Yea, the Saint is a strong Redeemer; the Spirit of God striveth within him.

34. And God withstandeth not God; for Love and God are One.

35. As the Love of Christ hath Power with the Elect, so hath Power in its degree the Love of a Man for his Friend.

36. Yea, though the Soule beloved be little and mean, a Creature not made in the Likenesse of Men.

37. For in the eyes of Love there is nothing little nor poor, nor unworthy of Prayere.

38. O little Soule, thou art mighty if a Child of God love thee; yea, poor and simple Soule, thou art possessed of great Riches.

39. Better is thy Portion than the Portion of Kings whom the Curse of the Oppressed pursueth.

40. For as Love is strong to redeem and to advance a Soule, so is Hatred strong to torment and to detain.

41. Blessed is the Soule whom the Juste commemorate before God; for whom the Poor and the Orphan and the dumb Creature weep.

42. And thou, O Righteous Man, that with burning Love bewailest the Death of the Innocent, whom thou canst not save from the Hands of the Unjuste;

43. Thou who wouldst freely give of thine own Blood to redeem thy Brother and to loosen the Bonds of his Paine;

44. Know that in the Houre of thy supreme Desire, God accepteth thine Oblation.

45. And thy Love shall not return unto thee empty; according to the Greatnesse of her Degree, she shall accomplish thy Will.

46. And thy Sorrowe and Teares, and the Travaile of thy Spirit, shall be Grace and Blessing to the Soule thou wouldst redeem.

47. Count not as lost thy Suffering on behalf of other Soules; for every Cry is a Prayere, and all Prayere is Power.

48. That thou willest to do is done; thine Intention is united to the Will of Divine Love.

49. Nothing is lost of that which thou layest out for God and for thy Brother.

50. And it is Love alone who redeemeth, and Love hath nothing of her own."

BENEDICTION

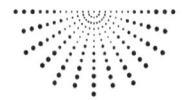

"May this holy Body and Blood, Substance and Spirit, Divine Mother and Father, inseparable Duality in Unity, given for all creatures, broken and shed and making oblation for the world, be everywhere known, adored and venerated! May we, by means of that Blood, which is the Love of God and the Spirit of Life, be redeemed, indrawn and transmuted into that Body which is pure Substance, immaculate and ever virgin, express Image of the Person of God!

That we hunger no more, neither thirst any more; and that neither death nor life, nor angels, nor principalities, nor powers, nor things present, nor things to come, nor height, nor depth, nor any creature, be able to separate us from the Love of God, which is in Christ Jesus.

That being made one through the At-one-ment of Christ, Who only hath Immortality and inhabiteth Light inaccessible; we also, beholding the Glory of God with open face; may be transformed into the same Image, from glory to glory, by the power of the Spirit."

Copyright © 2021 by Alicia Editions
All rights reserved.
Credits: Canva.com
No part of this book may be reproduced in any form or by any electronic or mechanical means, including information storage and retrieval systems, without written permission from the author, except for the use of brief quotations in a book review.

www.ingramcontent.com/pod-product-compliance
Lightning Source LLC
LaVergne TN
LVHW012127070526
838202LV00056B/5892